McPHERSON'S MARRIAGE ALBUM

JOHN McPHERSON

ZondervanPublishingHouse

Grand Rapids, Michigan

A Division of HarperCollinsPublishers

Requests for information should be addressed to:
Zondervan Publishing House
Grand Rapids, Michigan 49530

Library of Congress Cataloging-in-Publication Data

McPherson, John, 1959–
    [Marriage album]
    McPherson's marriage album / John McPherson.
        p.   cm
    ISBN 0-310-53901-3
    1. Marriage—Caricatures and cartoons. 2. American wit and
humor, Pictorial. I. Title
    NC1429.M275A4   1991a
    741.5'973—dc20   90-39290
                                                           CIP

Many of the cartoons in this book originally appeared in The
Chronicle of Glen Falls, Yankee, Marriage Partnership, Physician's
Management, and The Saturday Evening Post. Thanks is ex-
tended to these magazines for their kind permission in allowing
us to reprint these cartoons.

Back Cover Photo by Steve Robb
Cover Design by Steve Allen

Printed in the United States of America

93 94 95 96 97 / CH / 10 9 8 7 6 5

For my wife, Laura.

Thanks Laura, Beth, Keith, Rick, Bob, Kay, Mom, and Dad for your input.

Special thanks to Mark Frost of The Chronicle who published my first cartoon and has given me constant encouragement.

Many thanks to the staff of Marriage Partnership for their ongoing interest in my work.

THE
EARLY YEARS

"SORRY. I FORGOT TO BRING A LADDER."

"I HAVEN'T GOTTEN TO THAT PART YET!"

"WE COULDN'T FIND ANY RICE SO WE'RE USING MASHED POTATOES INSTEAD."

BUDGET WEDDING PHOTOS

"SORRY, STEVE. IT LOOKS LIKE YOU'RE CLOSEST TO THE GARTER."

"DARLING, THERE'S SOMETHING YOU SHOULD KNOW ABOUT ME."

"ARE YOU SURE THIS IS THE HONEYMOON SUITE?"

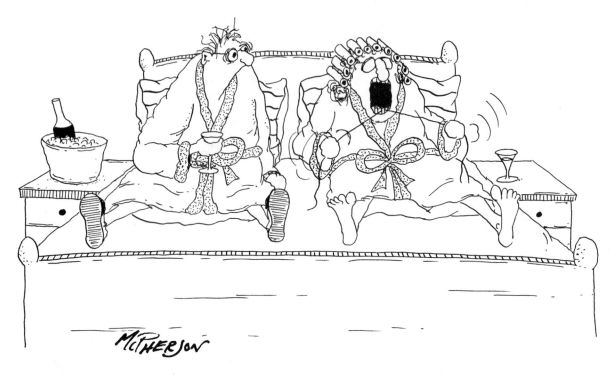

ONE OF THE 10 WARNING SIGNS THAT THE HONEYMOON IS OVER.

THE ULTIMATE IN TACKY THANK YOU NOTES.

BUD COMMITS ONE OF THE GRAVEST ERRORS
A NEWLYWED CAN MAKE.

MOST NEWLYWEDS HAVE A TENDENCY TO TRY TO AVOID CONFLICT.

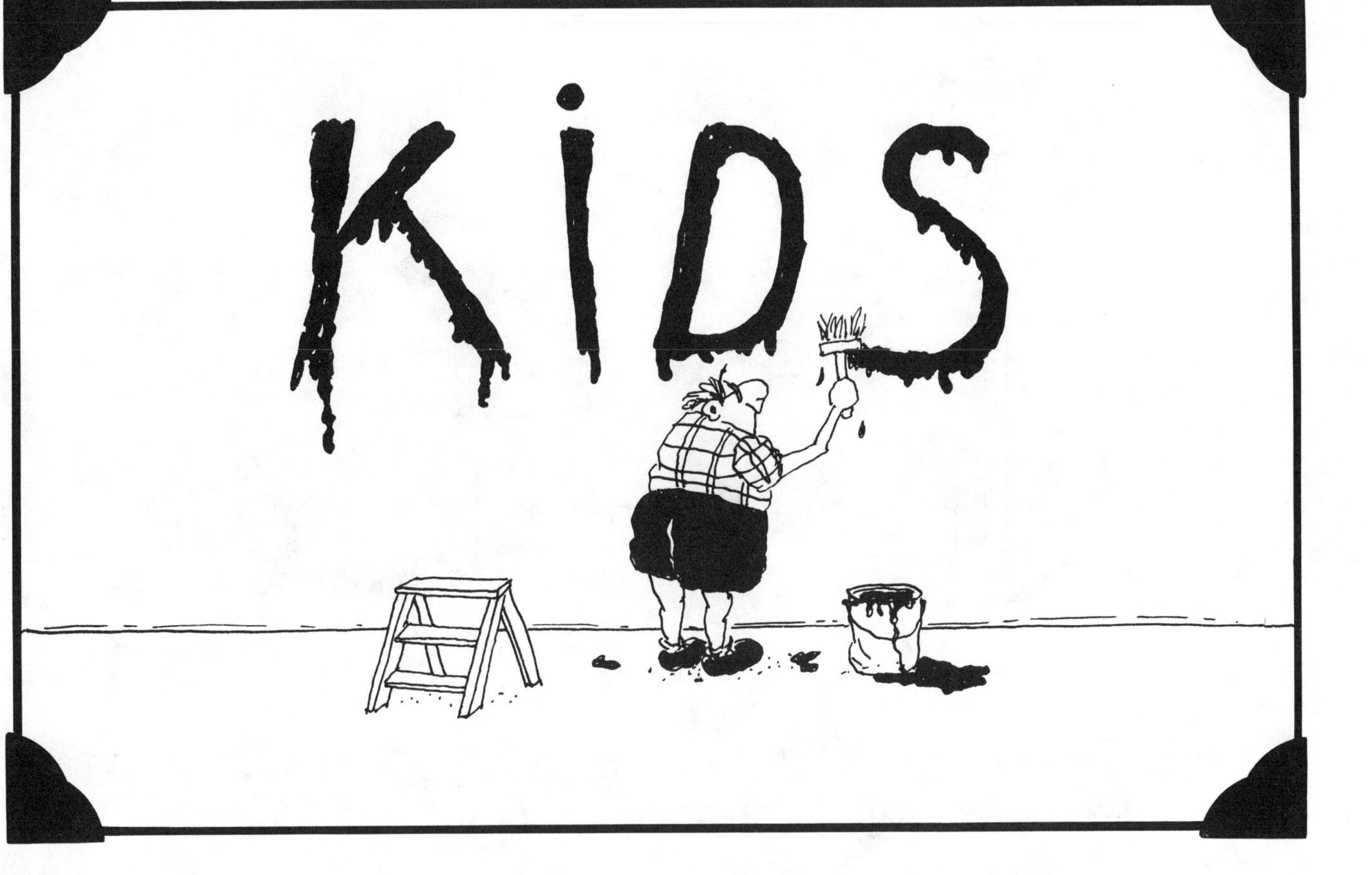
KIDS

"I DON'T CARE IF HE _WAS_ YOUR FAVORITE DOG. WE ARE _NOT_ NAMING OUR BABY 'OLD RED'!"

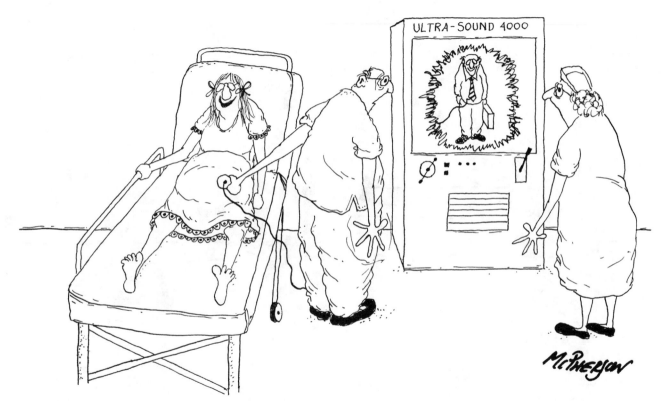

"WELL? WHAT IS IT? A BOY OR A GIRL?"

THE GROWING INTEREST IN HEALTH AND FITNESS HAS HAD AN EFFECT ON EVEN THE LONGEST STANDING OF TRADITIONS.

"I THINK YOU'RE SUPPOSED TO BE A LITTLE MORE SPECIFIC, FRANK."

ANXIOUS TO GET HIS SON STARTED ON SOLID FOODS, MARV ZEMBROWSKI CAME UP WITH THE LATEST BREAKTHROUGH IN CHILD CARE: BABY DENTURES.

"OH, HE LOOKS JUST LIKE HIS FATHER!"

"WELL, YOUNG MAN, IT LOOKS TO ME LIKE YOUR EYES WERE BIGGER THAN YOUR STOMACH."

"TELL US ABOUT THE TIME YOU BLOCKED THE FIELD GOAL AND SAVED THE BIG GAME AGAINST CORNELL, GRANDPA."

"GO TO YOUR ROOM!"

McPHERSON

"YOU CAN COME OUT NOW MRS. ZIFFLER. RON CAUGHT HOWIE AND LOCKED HIM IN HIS ROOM. SAY, IF YOU'RE NOT BUSY FRIDAY NIGHT WE'D LOVE TO HAVE YOU BABYSIT AGAIN."

MORT FELMLER WAS OBSESSED WITH WINNING THE $10,000 PRIZE ON AMERICA'S FUNNIEST HOME VIDEOS.

"BOYS WILL BE BOYS!"

MUSEUM OF CHILDREN'S ART

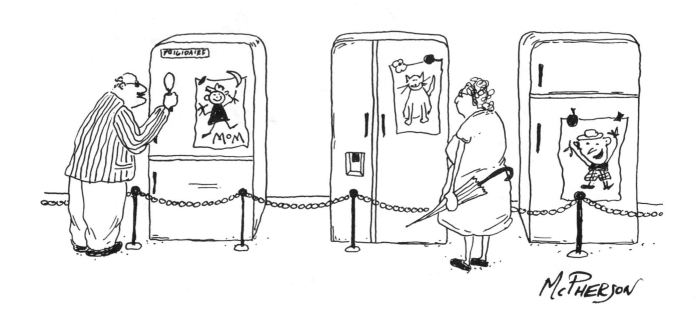

"ISN'T THAT CUTE? TOMMY'S BUILDING A TREE HOUSE."

"YOU KIDS DRIVE ME NUTS! ALL DAY LONG YOU PESTER ME ABOUT ICE CREAM AND NOW YOU AREN'T HUNGRY!"

"DAD, THE NINTENDO ISN'T TURNED ON. THAT'S 'WRESTLEMANIA' YOU'RE WATCHING."

"I'LL BE THERE IN A SECOND, DEAR.
I'M TUCKING THE KIDS IN."

"OH, LOOK AT THAT! FIRST A LAWN MOWER
AND NOW A SNOW SHOVEL! HOW ABOUT
A BIG 'THANK YOU' FOR YOUR FATHER, MARTY?"

"I'LL GIVE YOU FIVE BUCKS IF YOU'LL PUT EIGHT MILES ON THIS THING BEFORE YOUR FATHER GETS HOME."

PLAYING HOUSE

"VERN AND I HAVE DIFFERENT TASTES WHEN IT COMES TO DECORATING, BUT WE'VE BEEN ABLE TO COMPROMISE PRETTY WELL."

"THIS IS NOT WHAT I HAD IN MIND WHEN I SAID I WANTED US TO ADD A MASTER BATHROOM!"

"YOUR MOTHER? UH... NO. I HAVEN'T SEEN HER. I THINK SHE WENT FOR A WALK."

"THAT'S THE TV REMOTE CONTROL YOU'RE HOLDING,
NOT THE GARAGE DOOR OPENER."

McPHERSON

"I AM WAXING THE CAR! WHAT DOES IT LOOK LIKE I'M DOING?!"

"HOW MUCH LONGER ARE YOU GOING TO BE ON THIS DIET?"

"TRY JIGGLING THE HANDLE."

"CAN'T YOU DO SOMETHING ABOUT THIS STATIC CLING?"

"RALPH! WE'VE GOT A PROBLEM IN HERE WITH THE SPIN CYCLE!!"

"I THINK WE GOT A LITTLE CARRIED AWAY
WITH THE RUMMAGE SALE."

"GREAT JOB ON THE GARBAGE DISPOSAL, MR FIX-IT."

"ROGER, WE'VE BEEN OVER THIS BEFORE. I NEED MY CLOSET SPACE. BESIDES, THERE'S MORE ROOM FOR YOUR CLOTHES DOWN HERE."

JUST A TYPICAL MORNING FOR A ONE-BATHROOM COUPLE.

"ALL RIGHT, LEONARD. CAN YOU TELL ME WHICH PERSON TRACKED THE GREASE ONTO THE NEW CARPET? TAKE YOUR TIME."

"I INTERRUPT THIS PROGRAM FOR A SPECIAL ANNOUNCEMENT: GET OUT THERE AND MOW THE LAWN, DAVID!!"

"YOU DIDN'T HAPPEN TO SEE THE LID TO THE BLENDER COME THROUGH HERE, DID YOU?"

"AND THIS IS STAN'S PRIVATE LIBRARY."

"FOR HEAVEN'S SAKE! WILL YOU _PLEASE_ GO OUT AND BUY YOURSELF A _BLOWDRYER_?!"

"HE LEFT THE TOILET SEAT UP AGAIN."

"LET'S SEE. YOU'D TAKE A 36-INCH WAIST IN LONG UNDERWEAR, RIGHT?"

"LEO WANTED TO GET A HEAD START ON THE LEAVES THIS YEAR."

"WHILE YOU'RE IN THERE, ROGER, WHY DON'T YOU DUMP THOSE LEFTOVERS? SOME OF THAT STUFF IS STARTING TO LOOK PRETTY WIERD."

"YOU WOULDN'T BELIEVE THE MONEY WE SAVED BY BUYING REMNANTS."

"I SEE YOU HAD A LITTLE PROBLEM WITH THE WEED-EATER."

"WONDERFUL NEWS, GEORGE! YOUR COUSIN FREDDIE GOT A JOB SELLING VINYL SIDING!!"

"THANK HEAVENS THIS VACUUM HAS A REVERSE BUTTON!"

"I THINK YOU GOT THE BIRD SEED AND THE LAWN FERTILIZER MIXED UP AGAIN."

"WILL YOU QUIT SWEEPING THE DIRT UNDER THE RUG!!"

"HOWARD, I'M COLD. PUT ON TWO MORE CATS."

A
MEDLEY
OF
MARITAL
MADNESS

McPHERSON

"HAVE YOU TRIED BANGING ON HIS DINNER PLATE?"

"HOW MUCH DID YOU PAY FOR THESE BOX SEATS?"

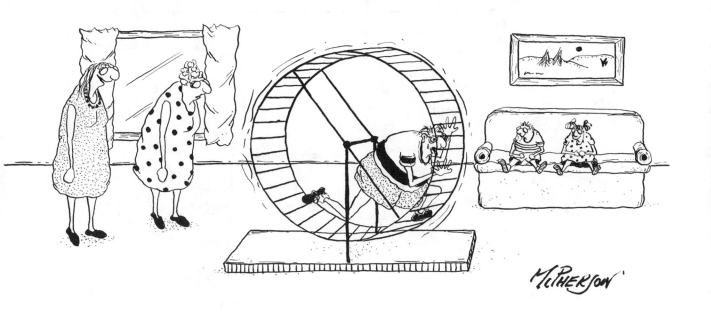

"NOT ONLY IS IT GOOD EXERCISE FOR BOB, IT'S ALSO GREAT ENTERTAINMENT FOR THE KIDS."

"FOR THE LAST TIME, WE ARE NOT BUYING AN EXERCISE BIKE!"

"HERE'S ANOTHER ONE OF ROWENA WAVING! THAT'S THE EIFFEL TOWER IN THE BACKGROUND AND IF YOU LOOK CLOSELY...."

"THEY'RE PERFECT, CHARLES! I'LL THINK OF YOU EVERYTIME I WEAR THEM."

MARGE AND STAN MURDOCK HAD WORKED OUT A SIGNAL TO LET EACH OTHER KNOW WHEN THE OTHER WAS SPENDING TOO MUCH TIME IN THE SHOWER.

NO SMOKING

"I WISH YOU'D RENEW YOUR MEMBERSHIP AT THE HEALTH CLUB."

"DON'T GIVE ME THAT OLD SONG-AND-DANCE ROUTINE!"

SNIP!

McPHERSON

HOW TO EMBARRASS YOUR SPOUSE.

"FOR PETE'S SAKE, STELLA, WATERBEDS ARE PERFECTLY SAFE!"

"HERE'S *THE PROBLEM*. THE BATTERIES TO THE GARAGE DOOR OPENER WERE IN BACKWARDS."

THE AGONY OF LIVING WITH
A COLD-FOOTED SPOUSE.

" I'M AFRAID WE CAN'T MAKE IT
TONIGHT, MADGE. LEO'S COME DOWN
WITH A CASE OF SWINE FLU. "

McPherson

"I THINK YOU'LL SORT OF GET A KICK OUT OF THIS WHEN I TELL YOU HOW IT HAPPENED."

"WHAT ARE YOU MAD AT ME FOR? YOU'RE THE ONE WHO BOUGHT ME THIS COLOGNE."

"SO YOU FOUND A GRAY HAIR. BIG DEAL!"

HOW TO STOP A BLANKET HOG

"I DON'T KNOW HOW WE GOT BY BEFORE WE HAD THE AUTOMATIC TELLER MACHINE INSTALLED."

A CURE FOR SNORING

FROZEN FOODS

McPHERSON

"APPARENTLY I HAVE DONE SOMETHING TO UPSET YOU."

"WHOOPS! SORRY I MISSED THAT REST AREA. OH, WELL, THE SIGN SAYS THERE'S ANOTHER ONE IN 76 MILES."

"TAKE THE NEXT RIGHT."

"OH, I'M SO GLAD YOU LIKE IT! I'M MAKING YOU A MATCHING PAIR OF PANTS IN QUILTING CLASS RIGHT NOW!"

"ARE YOU WEARING THAT MUSK COLOGNE AGAIN?"

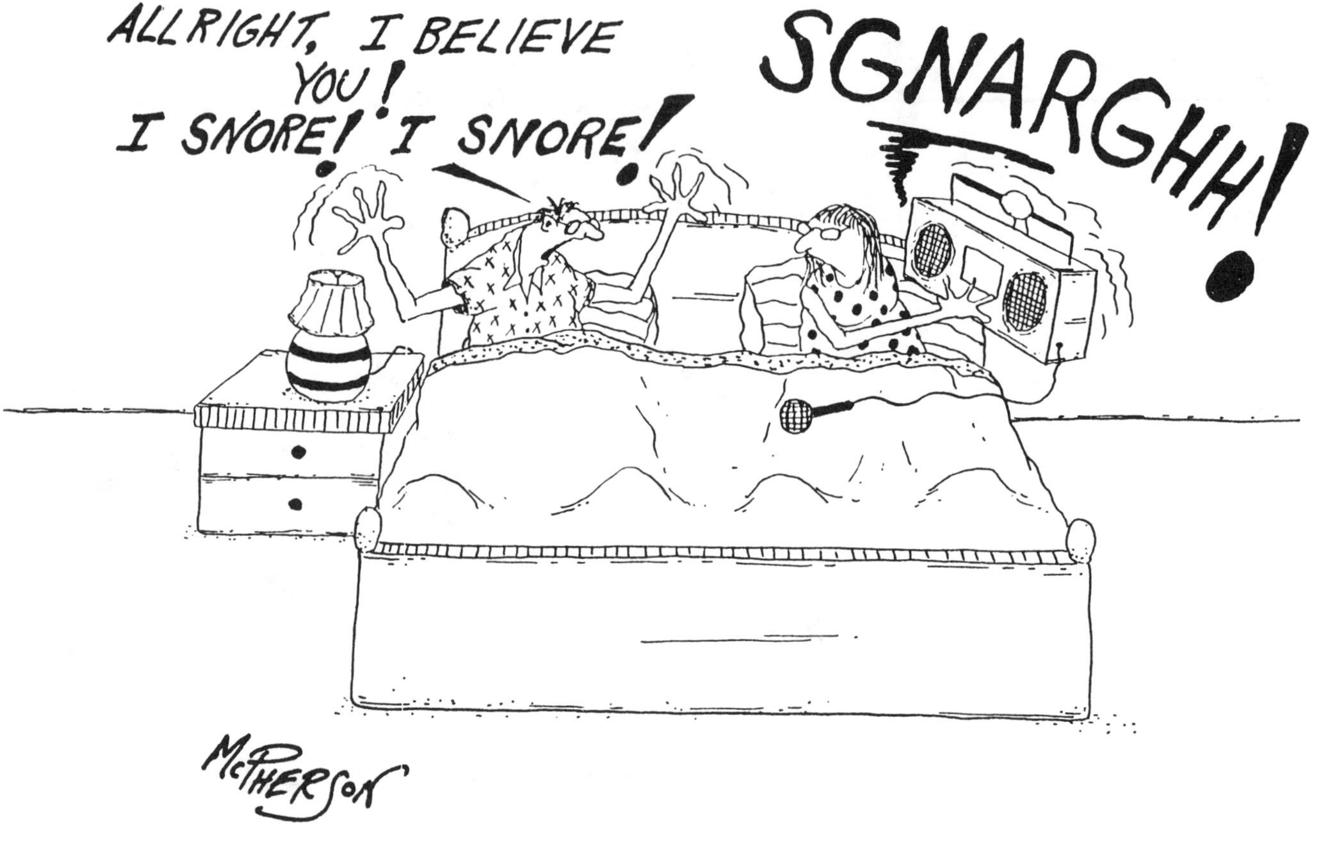
ALLRIGHT, I BELIEVE YOU! I SNORE! I SNORE!
SGNARGHH!
McPHERSON

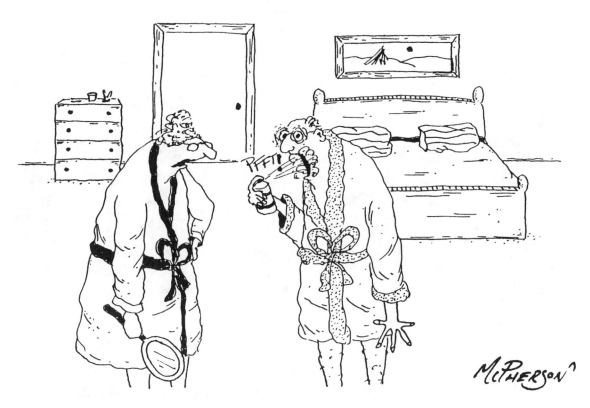

"THAT'S NOT YOUR BREATH SPRAY, IT'S YOUR DEODORANT."

"THIS ISN'T WHAT I WAS THINKING OF WHEN THEY INVITED US TO SEE THEIR SLIDES."

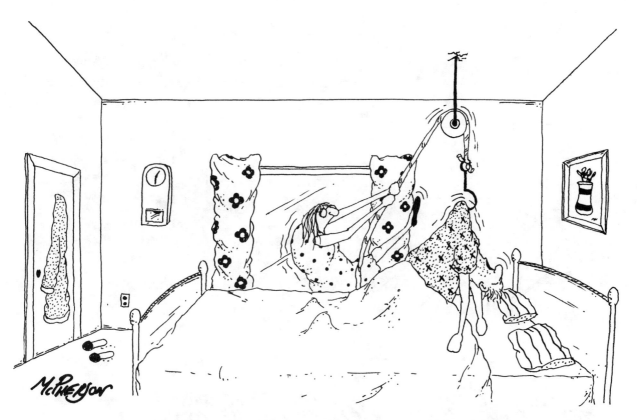

WALT NORDMAN WAS NOT A MORNING PERSON.

"WELL, MY HUSBAND AND I TALKED IT OVER AND AGREED THAT IT JUST ISN'T PRACTICAL FOR US TO OWN A SPORTS CAR SO WE DECIDED IT WAS BEST TO SELL IT."

"WILL YOU _PLEASE_ CUT YOUR TOENAILS ?!!"

"FOR THE ONE-HUNDREDTH TIME, I AM SORRY I USED YOUR NEW BATHROBE TO WAX THE CAR."

"THAT'S ONE OF THE THINGS I LOVE MOST ABOUT NORMAN.
HE'S A TERRIFIC LISTENER."

"I AM NOT PRIMPING! I JUST WANT YOU TO LOOK GOOD FOR YOUR MEETING. NOW LET ME FIX THIS COLLAR."

"RON, I KNOW YOU'RE FEELING A LITTLE SENSITIVE ABOUT YOUR BALD PATCH LATELY, BUT I REALLY THINK YOU'RE ONLY MAKING THE SITUATION WORSE."

"IT HELPS ME TO UNWIND."

NEVER LAUGH AT YOUR WIFE'S NEW HAIRDO.

"HIS HIGH SCHOOL REUNION IS IN TWO DAYS."

"OPERATOR, GET ME THE CHOCOLATE ABUSE HOTLINE!"